i can't believe i'm FREE-FORM CROCHETING

MEET
pamela pease

"My kindergarten teacher told my mom I would spend the rest of my life doing things with my hands. And she was right," says Pamela Pease.

There's certainly no disputing the teacher's prediction. Pamela's life has centered on creativity, and she began her working years in the floral industry.

"Working with flowers," says Pamela, "taught me how to see color, shape, and size. I learned how to use these features to make artistic compositions."

After 25 years of fashioning floral designs, Pamela became a buyer for a well-known needlework and crafts retailer that markets through catalogs and the Internet. In her free time, Pamela paints murals, works in her garden, and knits or crochets when and wherever she finds the time. "And I cook like a maniac," she confesses. "I also love creating things from items on hand, recycling whenever possible."

Now that Pamela's abundant energy and talent have extended to free-form crochet, readers everywhere can discover the quick and simple scrumbling shapes that form the basis of Pamela's designs.

"I like instant gratification projects," Pamela says. "I want easy projects that yield fast results."

And that's a design philosophy we can all appreciate!

WHERE TO FIND IT

motif gallery . . . . .pages 3-6
start to scrumble here . . . . . .pages 7-8

sampler scarf . . . . .pages 9-13

black bag map. . . . . .pages 14-15

project gallery. . . . . .pages 16-25
  yarn concho belt . . . . .page 16
  "disk-o" belt. . . . . .page 18
  pink handle purse . . . . .pages 20-22
  furry bag . . . . .pages 23-25

let's re-upholster a purse . . . .pages 29-33

general instructions . . . . . . .pages 34-38
  basic crochet stitches . . . . .page 36
  embroidery stitches . . . . . . .pages 37-38

credits . . . . .pages 38-39

Free-Form Crochet—it's an oddly contradictory term. "Free-form" sounds fluid and unshaped while crochet is rigidly controlled by rows and rounds and numbers—or is it? Because, once you get started with free-form crochet, you learn that:

- there are NO RULES!
- there is NO GAUGE!

Isn't that fabulous? However, for the sake of making it even easier to do, free-form crochet does have the *Scrumble*.

A "scrumble" is created by building stitches and motifs to other motifs until a fabric or form is made. Using a basic set of motifs as a starting point and then adding a couple of quick finishing techniques can result in fast and fabulous fashion.

So, if you can chain, single crochet, double crochet, half double crochet, work in the round, join with a single crochet, half double crochet or double crochet, then you are ready to do some serious scrumbling!

Next, check out all the fun shapes in our Motif Gallery!

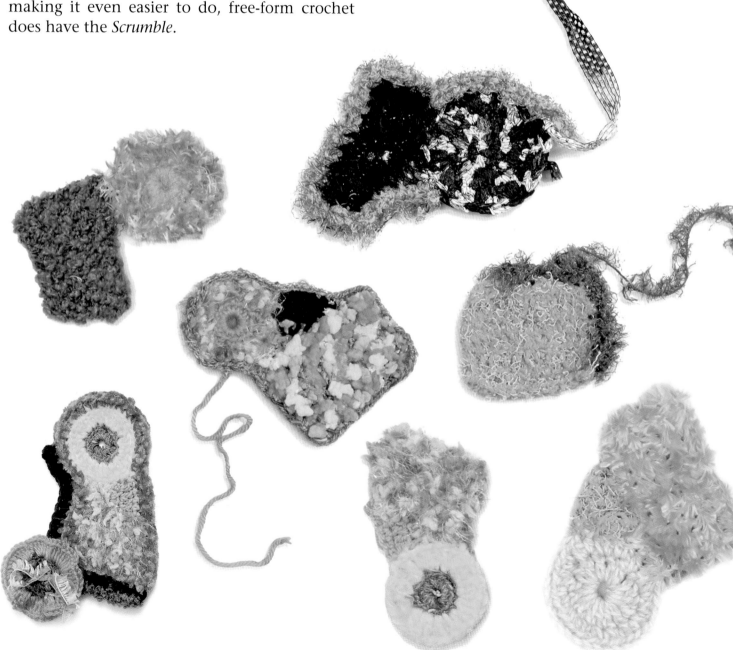

motif GALLERY

If you look closely at free-form crochet designs, you can spot basic patterns of circular and straight-edged motifs. You'll see everything from floral motifs and spirals to angles and wedge shapes. The following is just a small sample of what can be used.

FLAT flower

With first color, ch 5; join with slip st to form a ring.

Rnd 1 (Right side): Ch 2 (**counts as first hdc**), 15 hdc in ring; join with slip st to first hdc, finish off: 16 hdc.

Note: Loop a short piece of yarn around any stitch to mark Rnd 1 as **right** side. (This is our call for what is the "right" side. Decide for yourself which side you like better.)

Rnd 2: With **right** side facing you and working in Back Loops Only *(Fig. 2, page 35)*, join second color with dc in any hdc *(see Joining With Dc, page 34)*; dc in same st, 2 dc in next hdc and in each hdc around; join with slip st to first dc, finish off: 32 dc.

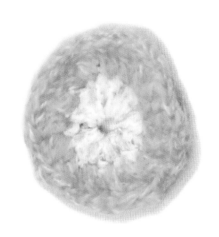

ROWS

(Use this to make square or rectangular space fillers.)

Chain a length that will fill an open area.

Row 1: Sc in second ch from hook and in each ch across.

Row 2: Ch 2 (**counts as first hdc**), turn; hdc in next st and in each st across.

Repeat Row 2 until your piece fits in the open area; finish off.

BUTTON flower

Ch 4; join with slip st to form a ring.

Rnd 1: Ch 3 (**counts as first dc**), 15 dc in ring; join with slip st to first dc, finish off: 16 dc.

Thread a yarn needle with a short length of bulky or super bulky weight yarn. Pull the needle up from the back side through one chain on the beginning ring and back down through a chain on the opposite side of the ring. Use the ends of the center yarn to sew the Button Flower down.

LOOPY flower

Loosely wrap yarn around the width of your fingers on one hand about 15 times or as many as you need. Slide the yarn off your fingers and tie a 12" (30.5 cm) length of yarn tightly around the center of the loops. Fluff the loops. Use the long ends of the center tie to sew the flower down.

PLATE

Ch 4; join with slip st to form a ring.

Rnd 1: Ch 3 (**counts as first dc**), 17 dc in ring; join with slip st to first dc, finish off.

Rnd 2: Join second color with hdc in any dc *(see Joining With Hdc, page 34)*; ch 1, (hdc in next dc, ch 1) around; join with slip st to first hdc, finish off.

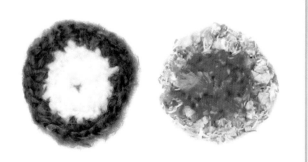

SPIRAL

(Especially super when made with a variegated yarn.)

Rnd 1: Ch 2, 4 sc in second ch from hook; do **not** join, place marker to mark beginning of rnd *(see Markers, page 35)*.

Rnd 2: 2 Sc in each sc around: 8 sc.

Rnd 3: (2 Sc in next sc, sc in next sc) around: 12 sc.

Rnd 4: ★ 2 Sc in next sc, working **around** next sc *(Fig. 4, page 35)*, sc in sc one rnd **below**; repeat from ★ around: 18 sc.

Rnd 5: Sc in each sc around.

Repeat Rnds 4 and 5 until the Spiral is the size desired or until you run out of yarn; do **not** join, finish off.

PETAL flower

Ch 4; join with slip st to form a ring.

Rnd 1: Ch 3 **(counts as first dc)**, 11 dc in ring; join with slip st to first dc.

Rnd 2: Ch 2, (dc, 2 hdc, slip st) in same st, ★ slip st in next 2 dc, (ch 2, dc, 2 hdc, slip st) in same st; repeat from ★ around to last dc, slip st in last dc; join with slip st to joining slip st, finish off.

RUFFLED flower

Ch 5; join with slip st to form a ring.

Rnd 1: Ch 2 **(counts as first hdc)**, 15 hdc in ring; join with slip st to first hdc: 16 hdc.

Rnd 2: Ch 3 **(counts as first dc)**, 2 dc in same st, working in Front Loops Only *(Fig. 2, page 35)*, 3 dc in next hdc and in each hdc around; join with slip st to first dc, finish off.

Rnd 3: Working in free loops of hdc on Rnd 1 *(Fig. 1a, page 35)*, join next color with slip st in any hdc; ch 3, dc in same st, 2 dc in next hdc and in each hdc around; join with slip st to first dc, finish off.

Ripple

(A tri-colored squiggle that will fill up bare little spaces.)

With first color, ch 21.

Row 1 (Right side): Sc in second ch from hook and in each ch across; finish off: 20 sc.

Note: Loop a short piece of yarn around any stitch to mark Row 1 as **right** side *(see Note on Flat Flower about "right" side)*.

Row 2: With **right** side facing you, join second color with sc in first sc *(see Joining With Sc, page 34)*; hdc in next sc, 2 dc in next sc, hdc in next sc, ★ sc in next 2 sc, hdc in next sc, 2 dc in next sc, hdc in next sc; repeat from ★ across to last sc, sc in last sc; finish off.

Trim: With **right** side facing you, join third color with sc in first sc; sc in each st across; sc in free loop of each ch across beginning ch *(Fig. 1b, page 35)*; join with slip st to first sc, finish off.

Dome

Rnd 1: Ch 2, 8 sc in second ch from hook; join with slip st to first sc.

Rnd 2: Working **around** the sts of the first rnd *(Fig. 4, page 35)*, 16 hdc in same ch as first rnd; join with slip st to first hdc, finish off.

ATTACHED rows

(This pattern can be attached to any piece on your project as long as you have 5 stitches free to be worked into for the first row. These particular set of instructions are written for the Attached Rows to be added to a Flat Flower.)

Row 1: With **right** side of Flat Flower facing you *(see Note on Flat Flower about "right" side)* and working in Back Loops Only *(Fig. 2, page 35)*, join yarn with hdc in any dc *(see Joining With Hdc, page 34)*; hdc in next 4 dc, leave remaining dc unworked: 5 hdc.

Row 2: Ch 7, turn; sc in second ch from hook and in each ch and each hdc across: 11 sc.

Rows 3-6: Ch 2 **(counts as first hdc)**, turn; hdc in next st and in each st across.

Finish off.

ANGLE

(Worked across two sides of the square or rectangle that the Rows pattern creates.)

Row 1: Working in sts on last row, join yarn with sc in first hdc *(see Joining With Sc, page 34)*; sc in each hdc across to last hdc, 3 sc in last hdc; sc in end of each row across.

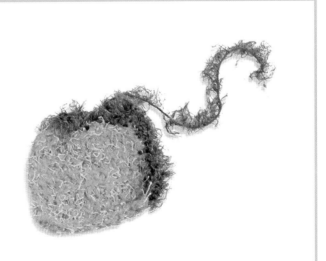

Rows 2-4: Ch 1, turn; sc in each sc across working 3 sc in center sc of 3-sc group.

Finish off.

WEDGE

(This little splash of color can be worked between any two pieces that meet at a pointy angle, like the one found between a Flat Flower and Attached Rows.)

Row 1: With **wrong** side of piece facing you, join yarn with slip st around last hdc on Row 1 of Attached Rows, ch 2 **(counts as first hdc)**; slip st in Front Loop Only of next st on Flat Flower, work 2 hdc around same hdc as joining slip st, slip st in beginning ch on Attached Rows.

Row 2: Ch 3 **(counts as first dc)**, slip st in beginning ch of Attached Rows, turn; dc in same st as last dc made, 2 dc in next hdc, dc in last hdc, slip st in Back Loop of next dc on Flat Flower.

Row 3: Ch 1, turn; sc in each dc across, slip st in beginning ch on Attached Rows; finish off.

OUTLINING

(Once the pieces are joined, use a yarn around them that makes them stand out. Unlike using crayons, you don't have to stay inside the lines as the curlicues on the Sampler Scarf show.)

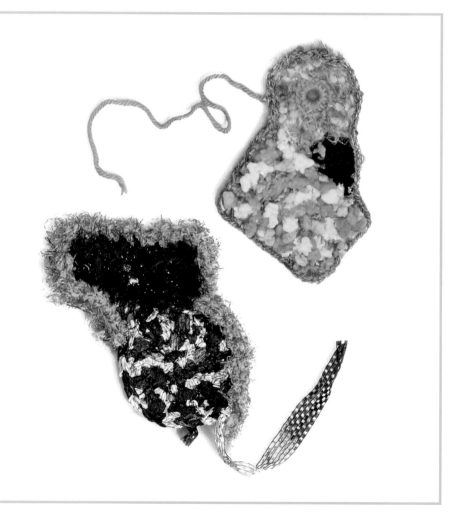

With **right** side of piece facing you *(see Note on Flat Flower about "right" side)*, join yarn with sc in any st or st specified in the following projects *(see Joining With Sc, page 34)*; sc evenly around, working in Back Loops Only on curved areas *(Fig. 2, page 35)* and in **both** loops elsewhere and working 3 sc in corners; either work completely around and join with slip st to first sc or stop at desired spot, finish off.

Pick up your hook and let's put it all together!
We used three large scrumbles—you can do any number you want.
Choose your favorite colors to make your own fashion statement.

What you will need:

Sport Weight Yarn:  **LIGHT 3**
  Green
  Red
  Purple
Medium Weight Yarn: **MEDIUM 4**
  Black
  Orange
Bulky Weight Yarn: **BULKY 5**
  Yellow
  Coral
  Bright Variegated Bouclé
  Orange/Pink Variegated
  Purple/Pink Bouclé
  Orange/Yellow Eyelash
Super Bulky Weight Yarn: **SUPER BULKY 6**
  Pink Chenille
Crochet hook, size H (5 mm)
Tapestry needle (for Sport Weight yarn)
Yarn needle (for heavier yarns)
Straight pins

REMEMBER - NO GAUGE: Your scarf can be bigger or smaller than our model depending on the yarns or hooks you use and how tightly or loosely you form your stitches. So jump right in and make the 1st Scrumble!

When a word is bolded like this—**Flat Flower**—it means that the instructions for that item can be found in Motif Gallery or Start to Scrumble Here, pages 3-8.

TURN THE PAGE FOR MORE.

1st SCRUMBLE

Begin a **Flat Flower** with Purple Sport Weight yarn, leaving a 15" (38 cm) end to be used for embroidery later.

Join Yellow Bulky Weight yarn with dc in any st *(see Joining With Dc, page 34)*; finish Flat Flower.

Join Orange/Pink Variegated Bulky Weight yarn with hdc in any dc *(see Joining With Hdc, page 34)*; work **Attached Rows**.

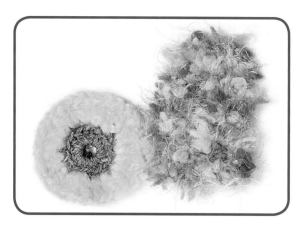

With Green Sport Weight yarn, work a **Wedge**, leaving a 15" (38 cm) end.

Use Purple Sport Weight yarn end to work a Lazy Daisy and a French Knot on Wedge *(see Embroidery Stitches, pages 37 and 38)*. Weave Green Sport Weight yarn end around top of every other dc on Rnd 2 of Flat Flower.

Join Pink Chenille Super Bulky Weight yarn with sc in the first unworked dc on Flat Flower after Wedge joining *(see Joining With Sc, page 34)*, work **Outlining**.

Join Black Medium Weight yarn with hdc in Back Loop Only of 20th sc on Outlining; hdc in each sc across to center sc of 3-sc group, 3 hdc in center sc, hdc in each sc across to center sc of next 3-sc group, hdc in center sc changing to Purple/Pink Bouclé Bulky Weight yarn *(Fig. 3, page 35)*; cut Black.

Ch 1, turn; sc in each hdc across to center hdc, (sc, ch 5, sc) in center hdc, **turn**; 15 hdc in ch-5 sp just made (center of Orange Flower); join with slip st to first hdc, finish off.

Join Orange Medium Weight yarn with dc in any hdc on Flower center; 3 dc in same st, 4 dc in next hdc and in each hdc around; join with slip st to first dc, finish off.

Pull a 12" (30.5 cm) length of Orange/Yellow Eyelash Bulky Weight yarn through Flower center; tie ends in a bow.

2nd SCRUMBLE

Work Rnd 1 of **Flat Flower** with Coral Bulky Weight yarn; then join Orange/Yellow Eyelash Bulky Weight yarn for Rnd 2 and finish Flat Flower.

With Pink/Purple Bouclé Bulky Weight yarn, work **Attached Rows**.

With Red Sport Weight yarn, work **Wedge**; do **not** finish off, continue to work sc across free loops of beginning ch of Attached Rows *(Fig. 1b, page 35)*, 3 sc in corner, sc evenly across end of rows, 3 sc in first hdc, sc in each hdc across.

Ch 1, turn; sc in each sc across to center sc of first 3-sc group you come to; do **not** finish off.

let's join them together into a MEGA SCRUMBLE!

Ch 1, turn; with **wrong** side of First Scumble facing you, matching sts, and beginning in corner hdc **behind** Orange Flower, sc in each st across; finish off. You will see that the "wrong" side of the 2nd Scrumble is on the same side as the 1st Scrumble's "right" side.

TURN THE PAGE FOR MORE.

OUTLINING the joined pieces

With the **right** side of the 1st Scrumble facing, join Yellow Bulky Weight yarn with sc in end of Red Sport Weight yarn row on 2nd Scrumble; sc evenly across end of rows and in Back Loops of dc on Flat Flower, sc in each Red Sport Weight st across to next corner sc, work 3 sc in corner sc, sc in next several sc until you have worked into a sc that is hidden by the Orange Flower, sc in next sc and catch a loop at back of dc on Orange Flower at the same time, ch 3, skip next 12 dc on Flower, slip st around loop at back of next dc, ch 3, working in Pink/Purple sts, sc in next hdc that shows from under the edge of the Orange Flower, sc in each hdc across to last hdc, 3 sc in last hdc, [ch 6, 3 sc in second ch from hook and in last 4 chs (**curlicue made**)], sc in end of Black row and in next 2 sc, work curlicue, (sc in next 3 sc, work curlicue) 4 times, sc evenly around; join with slip st to first sc, finish off.

Work **Button Flower** with Green Sport Weight yarn for Rnd 1 and Pink Chenille Super Bulky Weight yarn for center.
Sew Button Flower to Attached Rows on 2nd Scrumble.

3rd SCRUMBLE

Work Rnd 1 of **Flat Flower** with Orange Medium Weight yarn and leave a long end for embroidery stitching when finishing off. Join Orange/Pink Variegated Bulky Weight yarn, finish Flat Flower.

With Bright Variegated Bouclé Bulky Weight yarn, work **Attached Rows**.

With Black Medium Weight yarn, work **Wedge**.

Use the Orange Medium Weight yarn end to work Embroidery Chain St across Wedge.

Use Purple Sport Weight yarn for **Outlining**.

Pin 3rd Scrumble to 2nd Scrumble with Wedge at joining row of the 1st and 2nd Scrumbles and Flat Flower near Flat Flower on 1st Scrumble. With Green Sport Weight yarn, working through **both** thickness and **around** sc on Outlining of 3rd Scrumble, work slip stitch *(Fig. A)* to join the pieces, starting in center sc of first 3-sc group (next to Flat Flower on 2nd Scrumble) and ending in center sc of Outlining on Wedge; ch 12, 5 sc in second ch from hook and in each of next 7 chs, sc in next 2 chs, leave last ch unworked, finish off.

Fig. A

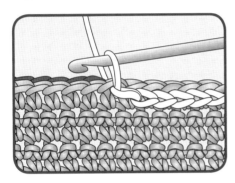

Now that you have the Scrumbles together, it's time to work the Scarf Foundation that allows you to wear your masterpiece.

SCARF FOUNDATION

Row 1: Join Black Medium Weight yarn with sc in corner sc of Outlining on 3rd Scrumble that has not been worked into yet, sc in each sc across to next corner sc (by 2nd Scrumble).

Row 2: Ch 14, turn; sc in second ch from hook and in each ch and each sc across.

To work beginning sc decrease, ch 1, turn; pull up a loop in first 2 sc, YO and draw through all 3 loops on hook (**counts as first sc**).

Row 3: Work beginning sc decrease, sc in each sc across.

Row 4: Ch 1, turn; sc in each sc across.

Repeat Rows 3 and 4 for pattern until 10 sc remain, then work without decreasing until Foundation measures approximately 36" (91.5 cm) long; finish off.

ADD A MOTIF

Work **Ruffled Flower** with Purple Sport Weight yarn for first 2 rounds and Pink Chenille Super Bulky Weight yarn for last round. Sew to Foundation above 3rd Scrumble.

With Black Medium Weight yarn, sew Outlining to edge of Foundation on each side of Flat Flower on 2nd Scrumble, leaving a 4" (10 cm) opening at top and leaving the 13 chains on Row 2 free. To wear, pull end of Foundation through the opening and under all the Scrumbles.

black bag MAP →

Every free-form project is a one-of-a-kind masterpiece. This bag is a perfect example. Your foundation purse will be a different size and/or shape than ours so it's impossible to give exact instructions. This "Map" identifies some of the elements used. This is what free-form is all about—use your imagination, your materials, and all the things you have learned in I Can't Believe I'm Free-Form Crocheting to create your own version.

angle

⚘ Remember all those gauge swatches you worked for past projects and set aside? Include the more interesting ones in your Scrumbles or rip them out to use the yarn.

loopy flower

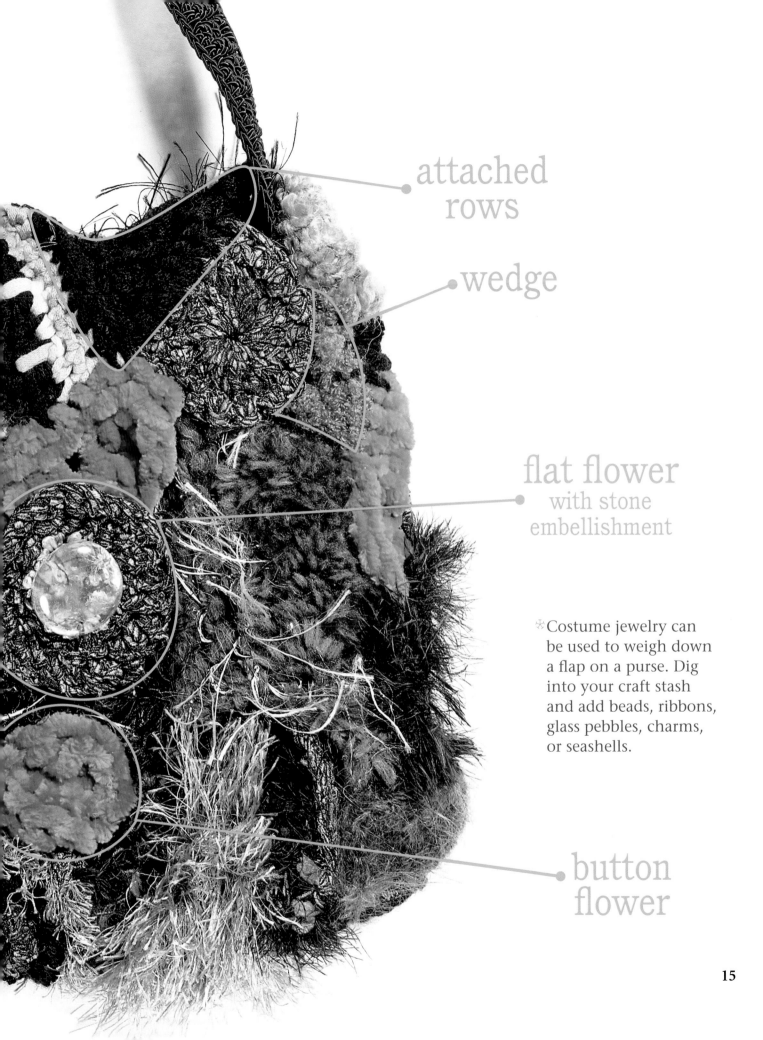

attached
rows

wedge

flat flower
with stone
embellishment

✳Costume jewelry can
be used to weigh down
a flap on a purse. Dig
into your craft stash
and add beads, ribbons,
glass pebbles, charms,
or seashells.

button
flower

15

project GALLERY

Look at all the things you can do with free-form crochet.

YARN GONGHO belt

Note: When a word is bolded like this—**Flat Flower**—it means that the instructions for that item can be found in the Motif Gallery, pages 3-6.

What you will need: Men's oversized belt, yarn, crochet hook, Velcro® fasteners, glue or hot glue gun and glue sticks.

Remove the prong from the belt buckle, but leave the buckle in place.

Glue one half of one Velcro® fastener to the back side of the belt under the buckle. Run the belt through the buckle until it's your size, then glue the other half of the fastener to the top side of the belt so the two parts meet. Glue another fastener to the spots where the tip meets the back side of the belt.

Once the fasteners are in place, work enough **Flat Flowers** to cover the length of the belt, using White for Rnd 1 and alternating Purple eyelash and ribbon yarns for Rnd 2.

Make a chain with Pink chunky yarn that is the same length as the belt plus some extra. Thread the chain through the centers of the Flat Flowers from the "wrong" side to the "right" side on each Flower.

Lay the belt on a flat surface. Pulling the extra length of chain through the buckle, arrange the Flat Flowers so that their edges are touching.

Glue the chain and all the Flowers down securely.

"DISK-O" belt

Notes: When a word is bolded like this—**Flat Flower**—it means that the instructions for that item can be found in the Motif Gallery, pages 3-6. The colors separated by a slash (/) will be a list of yarns in the order used for as many rounds as the item's instructions indicate; for example, **Flat Flower** -Black/Purple eyelash would mean that the first round of the Flat Flower will be Black and the last round will be Purple eyelash yarn.

What you will need: Men's oversized belt, old computer disk or DVD, large bead, yarn, crochet hook, Velcro® fasteners, glue or hot glue gun and glue sticks.

Work 2 **Flat Flowers**
   Black/Purple eyelash.
Work one **Flat Flower**
   Black/Variegated ribbon.
Work 2 **Plates**
   Pink/Variegated ribbon.

Wrap the computer disk or DVD with Purple chenille yarn until it is completely covered; glue the ends down. Glue the Black/Variegated Flat flower over the opening in the disk. Glue the large bead to the center of the Flat Flower with the hole in the bead running parallel to the disk. Thread a couple of lengths of ribbon yarn through the hole in the bead and tie ends in a knot.

Remove the prong from the belt buckle, but leave the buckle in place. Glue the wrapped disk to the top side of the buckle with one Pink Plate halfway under the disk and one Flat Flower underneath the Pink Plate. Leave the far edge of the Flat Flower free so you can glue it down over the belt cover later.

Glue one half of one Velcro® fastener to the back side of the belt under the buckle. Run the belt through the buckle until it's your size, then glue the other half of the fastener to the top side of the belt so the two parts meet. Glue another fastener to the spots where the tip meets the back side of the belt.

Once the fasteners are in place, glue the last Pink Plate and Flat Flower to the other side of the belt where it meets the buckle, leaving the far edge of the Flat Flower free as before.

With Black, make a chain to match the length of the belt that is not covered plus enough to go under the free edges of both of the Flat Flowers. Work single crochet rows until the piece is as wide as the belt; finish off.

Glue the cover to the belt, starting under the Flat Flowers on each side; then glue the Flat Flowers edges down to the cover.

PINK HANDLE purse

Notes: When a word is bolded like this—**Flat Flower**—it means that the instructions for that item can be found in the Motif Gallery or Start to Scrumble Here, pages 3-8. The colors separated by a slash (/) will be a list of yarns in the order used for as many rounds as the item's instructions indicate; for example, **Ruffled Flower** -White/ Purple eyelash would mean that the first 2 rounds of the Ruffled Flower will be White and the last round will be Purple eyelash yarn. Colors for the parts of the second Scrumble are inside the braces { }.

What you will need: Fabric or vinyl purse, fabric glue or hot glue gun and glue sticks, yarn, crochet hook, glass beads or desired embellishments.

SIDE one

Side One has two Scrumbles.
  Begin with **Flat Flower**:
    Dark Pink Chunky/White
    {Light Purple/Pink}.
  Add **Attached Rows** to the Flat Flower:
    Purple eyelash {Dark Pink Chunky}.
  Work a **Wedge** between the Flat Flower and the Attached Rows:
    Pink {Purple eyelash}.
  Work **Outlining** around the Scrumble:
    Light Purple {White}.
Side One also has a **Ruffled Flower** White/Purple eyelash.
  Knot six strands of Dark Pink eyelash in the center of the Flower.

TURN THE PAGE FOR MORE.

SIDE two

Side Two has one Scrumble.

Begin with a White/Light Pink **Flat Flower**.

With Light Purple, work **Attached Rows** to the Flat Flower.

Side Two has the following Flowers:

Work one **Flat Flower** in each of the colors below:

Pink/Dark Pink Eyelash

Dark Pink Chunky/Purple Eyelash.

Work 2 **Loopy Flowers** with Pink.

Side Two also has these motifs:

Work **Rows** with Pink, then add **Outlining** around Rows with White.

Work a **Ripple** with Pink/White/Purple eyelash.

END piece (Make 2)

Work **Rows** with Dark Pink Chunky.

Add **Outlining** with Pink.

Work two **Button Flowers** with White/Dark Pink Chunky.

Glue all pieces to purse, overlapping pieces and adding glass embellishments as desired.

FURRY bag

Notes: When a word is bolded like this—**Flat Flower**—it means that the instructions for that item can be found in the Motif Gallery or Start to Scrumble Here, pages 3-8. The colors separated by a slash (/) will be a list of yarns in the order used for as many rounds as the item's instructions indicate; for example, **Ruffled Flower** -White/Purple eyelash would mean that the first 2 rounds of the Ruffled Flower will be White and the last round will be Purple eyelash yarn. Colors for the parts of the second Scrumble are inside the braces { }.

What you will need: Fabric or vinyl purse, fabric glue or hot glue gun and glue sticks, yarn, crochet hook, glass beads or desired embellishments.

SIDE one

Side One has two Scrumbles.
> Begin with a **Flat Flower**:
>> White/Orange eyelash
>> {Pink/White}.
> Add **Attached Rows** to the Flat Flower:
>> White {Purple}
> Work a **Wedge** between the Flat Flower
>> and the Attached Rows:
>> Variegated {Orange fuzzy}.
> Side One also has two **Flat Flowers**.
>> Orange eyelash/Pink
>> Orange eyelash/Orange eyelash

Glue 1st Scrumble to the purse so that the Wedge and Flat Flower are on the bottom of the purse and Attached Rows are even with bottom edge.
Glue 2nd Scrumble overlapping the first one with Flat Flower at top edge of purse and Attached Rows are wrapping around to halfway cover the end piece.
Arrange Flat Flowers to cover areas not covered by the Scrumbles.

SIDE two

Side Two has one Scrumble:
> Flat Flower in White/Pink,
> Attached Rows in Orange fuzzy and
> Wedge in Orange eyelash.
Work **Rows** in White.

Glue White Rows to top edge of Purse.
Glue Scrumble over the White Rows with Flat Flower of Scrumble at top edge of Purse and Attached Rows wrapped around the bottom edge.
Leave end edge of Flat Flower free.

TURN THE PAGE FOR MORE.

END pieces

Work **Rows** to fit in the area:
    Purple - 2
    Pink - 1
    Work Flat Flower in Pink/White.

Glue one Purple end piece next to Attached Rows of Second Scrumble and wrapping around to White Rows on Side Two. Glue Flat Flower on top of Purple Rows.

Glue second Purple end piece to opposite end of Purse, next to Flat Flowers. Glue the Pink end piece at an angle on corner of Purse, on top of Flat Flower of the bottom Scrumble and second Purple piece and under Flat Flower of Side Two.

BOTTOM

Work one **Flat Flower** with White Variegated/Pink.
Work **Rows** in Orange fuzzy.

Glue Orange Rows to bottom of Purse.
Glue Flat Flower so that it overlaps the Rows and is halfway onto Side Two.

HANDLE

Cover handle by sandwiching it between two long **Rows**, Pink on underside and Orange fuzzy on top.

FUR

With White, work a **Loopy Flower**; cut loops and glue to top edge of Purse.
Repeat until top edge is covered completely.

Work **Flat Flower** in Pink/Purple and glue to Fur on Side One.
Add beads to centers of Flat Flowers as desired.

Remember, this book is all about setting your
IMAGINATION and CROCHET impulses free!

front

back

front

back

front

back

28

let's RE-UPHOLSTER a purse

Got a purse that you don't carry anymore because it's a little worn or its color doesn't match your wardrobe now? Give it a fashion facelift with Scrumbles.

Consider the shape of the purse you wish to cover to determine what motifs to make. Curves are a no-brainer with all the floral and circular motifs available. Straight edges can be matched with the beginning chain of a square or rectangle. Lay the Scrumbles down, arranging them to cover as much or as little of the area as you wish. Once you are satisfied with the pattern, sew the pieces together or glue them directly to the surface. You don't even have to cover both sides of the purse to give it a great new look.

Turn the page and SCRUMBLE together a purse!

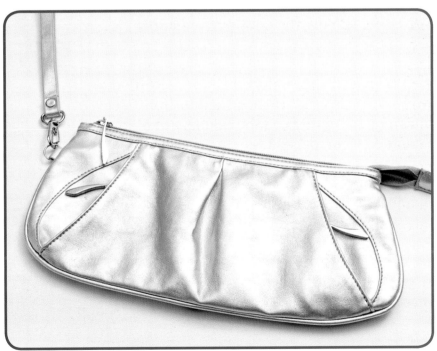

What you will need:

Light Weight Yarn:
   Blue Ribbon Yarn
Medium Weight Yarn:
   Blue
Bulky Weight Yarn:
   Blue Eyelash
   Navy Eyelash
Super Bulky Weight Yarn:
   Black Eyelash
   Black/Silver Ribbon
   Blue/Green Ribbon
#16 Silver metallic braid
Vinyl purse
Crochet hooks, sizes B (2.25 mm) (for braid),
   H (5 mm) (for Light and Medium Weight)
   and K (6.5 mm) (for Bulky and Super Bulky
   Weight)
Finishing materials: Fabric glue or hot glue
gun and glue sticks, sewing needle and
matching thread, beads or desired
embellishments.

This purse has hidden zippered side pockets. As we didn't want to lose the use of these, we are going to sew the Scrumbles together first, then sew the resulting "mega" Scrumble to the front of the purse, leaving the ends open to allow access to the pockets.

Note: When a word is bolded like this—**Ruffled Flower**—it means that the instructions for that item can be found in the Motif Gallery or Start to Scrumble Here, pages 3-8.

Since the purse has curved corners, let's start with a Black/Silver Ribbon **Spiral** for one corner. Work 6 rounds and finish off.

Work **Attached Rows** in Black Eyelash, joining in the 8th sc on the Black and Silver Spiral. Work 4 rows and finish off.

Work a **Wedge** with Blue Ribbon.

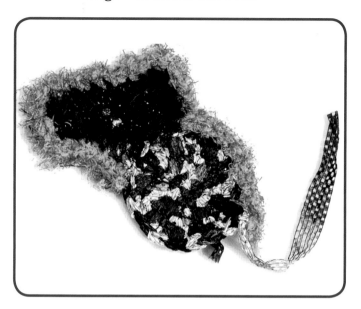

Work **Outlining** in Blue Eyelash, beginning in the first sc on the Spiral and ending with a slip st in same sc on the Spiral as the slip st on the Wedge. Leave a long end to stitch across the top of the Spiral.

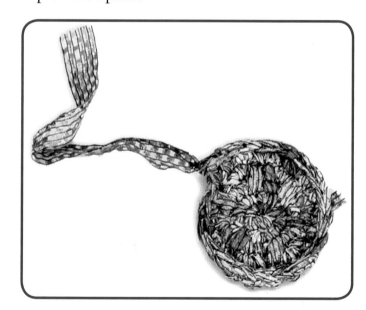

Work another Spiral with Blue/Green Ribbon with 5 rounds and finish off.

TURN THE PAGE FOR MORE.

Work a **Petal Flower** with Blue Ribbon. Sew to the Attached Rows.

Work a **Ripple** with the first row in Blue/Green Ribbon, the second row with Blue Medium Weight (use the same hook as the first row) and the Trim in Navy Eyelash. Work the Trim by joining on the **wrong** side, so you get the full benefit of the eyelashes when the Ripple is right side up.

Work two **Ruffled Flowers**, the first with Blue Ribbon for the first color and Blue Eyelash for the second color. For the second Flower, use one strand of Blue Ribbon with one strand of Blue Medium Weight held together for the first color (use largest size hook) and Black/Silver Ribbon for the second color.

With the silver braid, work a **Dome**. Sew this to the center of the second Ruffled Flower.

Work a **Loopy Flower** by wrapping a strand of Navy Eyelash and Blue Medium Weight around your fingers about 7 times.

With Blue Medium Weight, chain 20 and work **Rows** until the piece is about the same height as the purse from the edge of the zipper to the bottom, finish off.

With Navy Eyelash, chain 7 and work **Rows**. After 3 rows, finish off.

Arrange the pieces on the purse front with the large Blue Rows under most of the pieces and in the middle. Sew edges together that touch or overlap until the Scrumble is fairly solid. Using the sewing needle and thread, sew the Scrumble to the top and bottom edges of the purse, leaving the ends free (remember the pockets?).

Join Blue/Green Ribbon with sc around the purse strap, sc evenly across; finish off. Arrange the stitches so that the top looks like a braid.

Glue jewel to center of Blue/Green Spiral.

GENERAL instructions

ABBREVIATIONS

ch(s)	chain(s)
cm	centimeters
dc	double crochet(s)
hdc	half double crochet(s)
mm	millimeters
Rnd(s)	Round(s)
sc	single crochet(s)
sp(s)	space(s)
st(s)	stitch(es)
YO	yarn over

★ — work instructions following ★ as **many more** times as indicated in addition to the first time.

† to † — work all instructions from first † to second † **as many** times as specified.

( ) or [ ] — work enclosed instructions **as many** times as specified by the number immediately following **or** work all enclosed instructions in the stitch or space indicated **or** contains explanatory remarks.

colon (:) — the number(s) given after a colon at the end of a row or round denote(s) the number of stitches you should have on that row or round.

JOINING with SC

When instructed to join with sc, begin with a slip knot on hook. Insert hook in stitch or space indicated, YO and pull up a loop, YO and draw through both loops on hook.

JOINING with DC

When instructed to join with dc, begin with a slip knot on hook. YO, holding loop on hook, insert hook in stitch or space indicated, YO and pull up a loop (3 loops on hook), (YO and draw through 2 loops on hook) twice.

JOINING with HDC

When instructed to join with hdc, begin with a slip knot on hook. YO, holding loop on hook, insert hook in stitch or space indicated, YO and pull up a loop (3 loops on hook), YO and draw through all 3 loops on hook.

CROCHET TERMINOLOGY	
UNITED STATES	**INTERNATIONAL**
slip stitch (slip st) =	single crochet (sc)
single crochet (sc) =	double crochet (dc)
half double crochet (hdc) =	half treble crochet (htr)
double crochet (dc) =	treble crochet (tr)
treble crochet (tr) =	double treble crochet (dtr)
double treble crochet (dtr) =	triple treble crochet (ttr)
triple treble crochet (tr tr) =	quadruple treble crochet (qtr)
skip =	miss

Yarn Weight Symbol & Names	SUPER FINE 1	FINE 2	LIGHT 3	MEDIUM 4	BULKY 5	SUPER BULKY 6
Type of Yarns in Category	Sock, Fingering Baby	Sport, Baby	DK, Light Worsted	Worsted, Afghan, Aran	Chunky, Craft, Rug	Bulky, Roving
Crochet Gauge Ranges in Single Crochet to 4" (10 cm)	21-32 sts	16-20 sts	12-17 sts	11-14 sts	8-11 sts	5-9 sts
Advised Hook Size Range	B-1 to E-4	E-4 to 7	7 to I-9	I-9 to K-10.5	K-10.5 to M-13	M-13 and larger

CROCHET HOOKS													
U.S.	B-1	C-2	D-3	E-4	F-5	G-6	H-8	I-9	J-10	K-10½	N	P	Q
Metric - mm	2.25	2.75	3.25	3.5	3.75	4	5	5.5	6	6.5	9	10	15

MARKERS

Markers are used to locate the beginning of each round being worked. Place a 2" (5 cm) scrap piece of yarn before the first stitch of each round, moving the marker after each round is complete. Remove the marker when it's no longer needed.

FREE loops

After working in Back or Front Loops Only on a row or round, there will be a ridge of unused loops called the free loops. Later, when instructed to work in the free loops of that same row or round, work in these loops *(Fig. 1a)*. When instructed to work in free loops of a chain, work in loop indicated by arrow *(Fig. 1b)*.

Fig. 1a

Fig. 1b

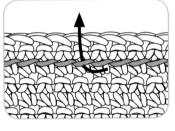
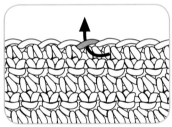

BACK or FRONT loop ONLY

Work only in loop(s) indicated by arrow *(Fig. 2)*.

Fig. 2

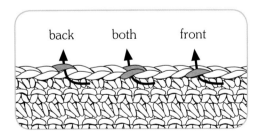

CHANGING colors

Insert hook in stitch indicated, YO and pull up a loop, drop yarn, with new yarn *(Fig. 3)*, YO and draw through both loops on hook.

Fig. 3

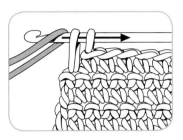

WORKING around a STITCH

Work in stitch or space indicated, inserting hook in direction of arrow *(Fig. 4)*.

Fig. 4

basic CROCHET stitches

CHAIN

To work a chain stitch, begin with a slip knot on the hook. Bring the yarn **over** hook from back to front, catching the yarn with the hook and turning the hook slightly toward you to keep the yarn from slipping off. Draw the yarn through the slip knot *(Fig. 5)* (first chain st made, *abbreviated ch*).

Fig. 5

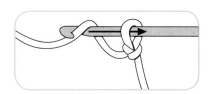

SLIP stitch

To work a slip stitch, insert hook in stitch indicated, YO and draw through stitch and through loop on hook *(Fig. 6)* (slip stitch made, *abbreviated slip st)*.

Fig. 6

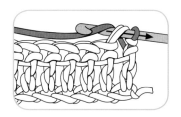

SINGLE crochet

Insert hook in stitch indicated, YO and pull up a loop, YO and draw through both loops on hook *(Fig. 7)* (single crochet made, *abbreviated sc)*.

Fig. 7

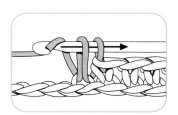

HALF DOUBLE crochet

YO, insert hook in stitch indicated, YO and pull up a loop, YO and draw through all 3 loops on hook *(Fig. 8)* (half double crochet made, *abbreviated hdc)*.

Fig. 8

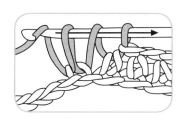

DOUBLE crochet

YO, insert hook in stitch indicated, YO and pull up a loop (3 loops on hook), YO and draw through 2 loops on hook *(Fig. 9a)*, YO and draw through remaining 2 loops on hook *(Fig. 9b)* (double crochet made, *abbreviated dc)*.

Fig. 9a   Fig. 9b

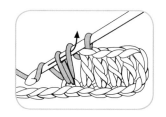 

TREBLE crochet

YO twice, insert hook in stitch indicated, YO and pull up a loop (4 loops on hook) *(Fig. 10a)*, (YO and draw through 2 loops on hook) 3 times *(Fig. 10b)* (treble crochet made, *abbreviated tr)*.

Fig. 10a   Fig. 10b

EMBROIDERY stitches

BACKSTITCH

The backstitch is worked from **right** to **left**. Come up at 1, go down at 2 and come up at 3 *(Fig. 11)*. The second stitch is made by going down at 1 and coming up at 4.

Fig. 11

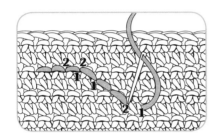

CHAIN stitch

Chain Stitch is worked from right to left. Make all stitches equal in length. Come up at 1 and make a counterclockwise loop with the yarn. Go down at 1 and come up at 2, keeping the yarn below the point of the needle *(Fig. 12a)*. Make a loop with the yarn and go down at 2; come up at 3, keeping yarn below the point of the needle *(Fig. 12b)*. Secure last loop by bringing yarn over loop and down.

Fig. 12a

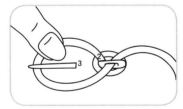

Fig. 12b

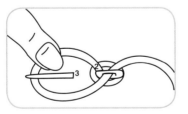

FRENCH knot

Bring needle up at 1. Wrap yarn around the needle the desired number of times and insert needle at 2, holding end of yarn with non-stitching fingers *(Fig. 13)*. Tighten knot; then pull needle through, holding yarn until it must be released.

Fig. 13

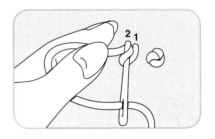

LAZY DAISY stitch

Make all loops equal in length. Come up at 1 and make a counterclockwise loop with the yarn. Go down at 1 and come up at 2, keeping the yarn below the point of the needle *(Fig. 14)*. Secure loop by bringing thread over loop and down at 3. Repeat for the desired number of petals or leaves.

Fig. 14

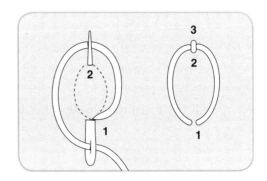

OUTLINE stitch

Bring needle up at 1, leaving an end to be woven in later. Holding yarn **above** with thumb, insert needle down at 2 and up again at 3 (halfway between 1 and 2) *(Fig. 15a)*; pull through. Insert needle down at 4 and up again at 2, making sure yarn is **above** needle *(Fig. 15b)*; pull through. Continue in this manner.

Fig. 15a

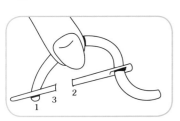

Fig. 15b

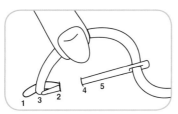

SATIN stitch

Satin Stitch is a series of straight stitches worked side-by-side so they touch but do not overlap. Come up at odd numbers and go down at even numbers *(Fig. 16)*.

Fig. 16

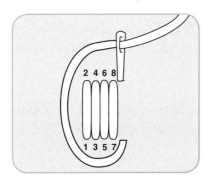

STRAIGHT stitch

Straight stitch is just what the name implies, a single, straight stitch. Come up at 1 and go down at 2 *(Fig. 17)*.

Fig. 17

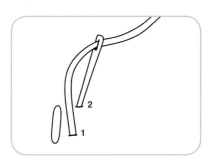

TURKEY LOOP stitch

This stitch is composed of locked loops. Bring yarn needle up through a stitch and back down through same stitch (Point A, *Fig. 18*) forming a loop on **right** side of work. Insert needle up through stitch to either side of loop (Point B), back down through Point A, and back up through Point B. Begin next stitch at Point B.

Fig. 18

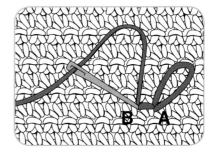

We would like to thank the following companies for providing yarn for the projects in this leaflet:

Mary Maxim®   Lion Brand®
Caron International®   Spinrite®
Coats & Clark®

✳ The quickest way to get great results is to hot glue or sew scrumbles to a foundation.

✳ By using a purse, tote, or belt as your foundation, you'll discover that free-form crochet is a fast and fun way to use your yarn stash while creating something new out of something old.

Use this for INSPIRATION for your own free-form crochet. HAPPY SCRUMBLING!

We have made every effort to ensure that these instructions are accurate and complete. We cannot, however, be responsible for human error, typographical mistakes, or variations in individual work.

Production Team: Instructional Editor - Sarah J. Green; Technical Editor - Linda Luder; Editorial Writer - Susan McManus Johnson; Graphic Artist - Dayle Carozza; Senior Graphic Artist - Lora Puls; Photo Stylist - Angela Alexander; and Photographers - Jason Masters and Ken West.

ISBN 1-60140-127-2